The Salt Flowers

The Salt Flowers

poems by **Travis Ian Smith**

MTPages • Houston, Texas

Published by MTPages
3514 Corondo Court, Houston, Texas 77005, USA

Cover design: Samantha Scheel

Copyright © 2010 by Travis Ian Smith. All rights reserved. Manufactured in the United States of America. Except in the case of brief quotations in reviews, no part of this publication may be reproduced or transmitted in any form or by any means without written permission from the author or publisher. This is a work of poetry; any resemblance to actual events or persons is entirely coincidental.

First Edition

Library of Congress Control Number: 2009944178

ISBN 978-0-615-34541-3

for Boo

Contents

Grace   17

Window in Nice, 1919   18

Giant, Red Hibiscus   19

The Salt Flowers   20

The Rosebush   21

Boulevard   22

Self-Portrait, 2006   23

Sunset, Corpus Christi   24

Ars Poetica   26

Jeweled String   27

What Spiders Do   28

Remembering the Water Burial   29

Still Life with Boy and Trees   31

Portrait of Sleeping Lovers   32

Big Sur   33

Hotel Galvez   34

Ovid's Narcissus   35

The Blue Room   36

Sojourn   37

At the Port House   38

Amulet   41

Continuum   42

Annunciation Street   43

Self-Portrait in New Orleans   44

November Days   46

The Snowflake   47

Lafayette Cemetery No. 1   48

Come   49

First Lines of an Unfinished Elegy   50

The Many Stars   51

Horses of Cerrillos   52

That Other River   54

Snow   55

Early Morning, Winter   56

The Junkyard   57

Seven   60

House   61

Seascape   63

Mythic Fragment   64

The Missing One   65

Nude Blue III, 1952   66

The Sleepers   67

Reckonings   68

Now Many Days   69

To Borges   71

La Nouvelle Orleans   73

Marine   74

Acknowledgments

Grateful acknowledgment is made to the following publications, in which some of the poems in this book first appeared: *Red River Review, The Grasslands Review, The Texas Observer, Borderlands: Texas Poetry Review, Persona, Sun Poetic Times, The Phoenix, Volpe*, and *The Austin Chronicle*

"Giant, Red Hibiscus" was also published in the anthology *Is This Forever, Or What?": Poems and Paintings from Texas* by HarperCollins, 2003

"Come" also appeared in a broadside published by Baylor University acknowledging the First Annual Beall Poetry Festival

My gratitude as well to the Sewell Elam Foundation in Austin for its generous support while writing this manuscript

Vast and starless, the pall of heaven
Laps on the trailing pall below;
And forward, forward, in solemn darkness,
As if to the sea of the lost we go.

—Walt Whitman

from "Sailing the Mississippi at Midnight"

The Salt Flowers

Grace

Like one beloved bead on a rosary's crimson string. The warmth
of the sun passing through the window onto the blind man's forearm.
He listens to her outside in the garden planting next summer's lilacs.
He dreams it all up again: last night's heavy cloth laid on the table,
the dry red wine, her spooning the fried duck into his mouth for him.
And the huge white rose she cut for him held in his palm like love,
its deep folds like the layers of her clothes, the rumpled bed.
Grace is the moment when she enters the room
and her hand which brushes his neck as she walks by.

Window in Nice, 1919
(Matisse)

No, I painted this one from memory. Once, years ago,
in Nice, I stood before that window, for hours,
heart-broken, holding a telegram announcing
the death of a friend, a lover actually.
Even though I no longer remember her face
or the sound of her voice, I remember
that room, that day, the open window,
how the tulips on the table were beginning to bloom,
how the salty air blew in from the sea,
across my face, and how, one after another,
strangers strolled by like shadows
on their way to work or to the beach.
Picasso said it's how memory works,
how the mind governs the heart. But that world
came back to me. First the window, then the sea, the colors.
Then she did. Then I did.

Giant, Red Hibiscus

I wish you were here waiting with me in my mother's garden.
The early morning sunlight has splintered
through the fence, has every leaf glittering.

I am waiting for the giant, red face of the hibiscus to open.

And I would like to watch you watch the hibiscus
in early morning,
how it changes from some seemingly red, dead-looking thing
into the most beautiful bloom on earth.

How many times have you said
that I never share anything with you,
that I never tell you what's important to me?
Well, here it is. The hibiscus, I mean.

When I saw it yesterday for the first time I remembered difficulty.
And I wanted you to see it.

I wanted us to watch something open and not be afraid.

The Salt Flowers

I don't know why something in me
closes like hands
in these days of June

I don't know turning above
everything at night
the endless braid of stars

I don't know flowers or rain or nightmares
or the unraveling thread that is
my future

It is Sunday
The heat rises into pearls

I remember
daylight twisted in palm trees
clouds reflected on the sea

Your mouth embroidered with mine

The Rosebush

does not resemble us   by the west wall illuminated

with its pink yield   little wheels

four inches small   in diameter

sometimes I prefer to see   only the blossoms

floating there   sometimes I remove the bush

and see only   the blossoms

floating   by the garden wall

tendrils in sunlight   in heavy clusters

little red explosions   in the yard

and their bodies go   wildly in the air

bursting and opening   into fires

like bandages   stained with blood

Boulevard

By the sun-accustomed street in the populous city
past the endless hands of silk merchants, flower vendors
a string of lilies   a crucifixion of roses

What I love I will not possess in death

On Monday sunset in the plaza, in her hand a small cup of light
Tuesday rain she waited under the flying blossoms
of mimosa trees Wednesday she wore a scarf of fragile green

Or three ballerinas ascending a narrow staircase to the fifth floor
of a stone building

>   they twirl beneath florescent lights
>   they are endlessly erotic
>   they are clouds

Or five nuns moving up traffic past the Cathedral

>   they are five hearts of flame
>   they are five lilies bent towards the Sun

I go up Guadalupe in my dark suit
& I too would like to be quiet and holy as clouds

Self-Portrait, 2006

When I am illuminated, shined on by a light,
it is only my darkness that is lit,
and when night comes
with its blue hook
it is only my light that has become faded

In the maelstrom of my myself
I live in two worlds

Both light and shadow
faith and doubt
yearning and indifference

So that I know
grace from a fallen state

So that your beauty is also
my suffering

And fire, like your tongue, burns me
when I'm already ash

Sunset, Corpus Christi

The sun
giant red colossus

as it slides
into the sea

burning still
its lower half

melted across the surface
pink watery flame

vermillion ships
burning on

the far horizon
auburn weeds

skimmering
across the tide

the rosy shards
of a broken bottle

glinting
in the sand

everything
smeared in red

except the white star
rising over

Ars Poetica

Is the acquisition of wings possible except through language?
Shall we say the world is a house full of white flowers

in simple poems, and hang them like paintings on every wall
so that we live in a world like a house full of flowers?

Silver moonlight comes in through the open window,
bright butterflies land in our open palms.

Ah, to write the largest object of desire in order to have it—
a woman bathing in sunlight, a pandemonium of flowers

overtaking the house; a father becoming the sparrow on the branch;
a sonnet wherein you become the evening star

climbing the fallen scene of night; a lyric poem
that captures your life in an image: a blossoming tree

stripped by wind and rain. Poetry is your life:
ascend and vibrate like a reed from all depths.

Jeweled String

Then one morning I could not pass the five nuns
standing at the corner in watery brightness and flame.
Nor could I have waited any longer
for the bleached white light to gather in palm trees
like suns evaporating my eyes. And the blue bouquet of hydrangeas
wilting under the breaths of shirtless men,
and the avenue of darkened women pressing white buds of camellias
into their braids of silken hair. High up in the branches
of the honey locust trees, a red cardinal
in the sun-splotched leaves is like a boy dropping
yellow petals of daisies into a fountain of water.
I turn up Twenty-third Street
past red walls of tomatoes, baskets of tuna, eels,
the way clouds rise from their split cocoons, the way a spider
hangs a filament high between two peach trees, the way men become
flowers in the mouths of the nuns, and somewhere inside myself
five little hearts begin to kneel.

What Spiders Do

I remember a friend driving through a countryside
in the early morning, a light frost making the landscape turn whitish-gold,
all glitter: the windshield, the road, the trees.
Then suddenly he saw braids of light flowing through the air,
making a crystal pattern between trees, connecting them,
hundreds of spider webs illumined in air,
visible for a second or two. This is how I remember
the sea horse at the city aquarium: as a thing
fragile, momentary, of beauty. I saw the infinite flowers
it carried on its back, the delicate shields
fashioned across its body. Or once I was enamored watching a woman
walking through an empty restaurant
at midnight, blowing out
the twenty candles. She did it
silently, diligently, bowing down before each flame
and moving on
with such severe indifference.
Or those twelve white cactus flowers I watched open
one summer, late at night,
bringing the bats.
There is nothing so heavy in this world
as beauty
passing through.

Remembering the Water Burial

for my sister

Under water
the silence
that holds you
& disarms you
is a rehearsal
for death
& those summer evenings
we wore
the water
like a dress
plunging
into bottomless lakes
or rivers
with so much
blue water
to kick in
we'd watch
the first stars appear
in the blue
pink
orange
red sky
as the sun collapsed
above canyons
then run home

in darkness
freezing
in our pruned skin

Still Life with Boy and Trees

Now a young boy sleeping beside a green river.
Water lilies on the surface reflecting yellow light.
On a rock he sleeps, curled, on his side,
like a Z. His bronzed right arm flung over his head,
legs bent at the knees and kicked out behind him.
And the delicate wind stirring the brown hair from his eyes
is like a wife's hand, years later, lifting him from another sleep.
And the long, plaintive notes from a nearby heron
descending into his body. In his dream,
he sees a wren spiraling among leaves, then
he is holding an endless piece of blue string.
He drifts back and forth, in and out of sleep.
Above him, a blue towel hung inside a tree,
a slanted magical light striking the dark leaves.

Portrait of Sleeping Lovers

Outside, the orange trees dangle tiny leaves reflecting silver light.
White noon, white April. And the whitened curtain lifted
by a small breeze, exposing two sunflowers in a mason jar.

On the disheveled bed they sleep, bodies intertwined.

She is dreaming of horses passing in a field of clover.
He is falling through the green depths of the sea.

Above them, one filament hangs from the ceiling
from a spider now no more. A light mist falls on the oranges,
which are star-like, and heavy in the trees.

Big Sur

Waves urchins sandpipers   the sun a lilac-colored flame
shrouded in pink mist
                         I was in love with a woman
whose eyes hoarded the blue flowers of the South

Over the grassy floor waves of white water
crashed against black cliffs
sending up low clouds of salt

I saw woven strands of light   clouds reflected on the sea

Wave after wave   *I was ashes*

Hotel Galvez

The sea was stained and white and lovely,
but something happened (a sudden sadness, a premonition of death)

as he watched the waves dismantle an abandoned sandcastle.
One belief said that all souls pass into a river of light,

a river made of specks and dust and prisms, our lives
no longer temporal, and we go on; while another said

that we exist like a flame between two fingers closing in on it,
that there is no other shore, and that death is final.

But the thought kept growing in him. He did not want to die.
A few shorebirds gathered on a pier; the sandcastle was hardly discernible now.

Perhaps he knew that what he wanted was found in this world only—
in the body of the woman that he brought his mouth to,

in the littered and dirty harbor where he walked and thought,
where the sea sprayed flowers and a sand dollar was found broken in half.

He began his journey home; two birds identical in the summer twilight
sailed up and over the roof of the white hospital.

Ovid's Narcissus

Beautiful Narcissus, drowned boy, the sea suffers desire,
    and the aged, tireless way the ocean throws itself upon darkened sand

with so much white light, fuss, and spray,
    to no entrance, or end, resembles your desire.

Your eyes like twin dazzling stars loved his recognizable face:
    When my lips go down to kiss the pool, his rise, he reaches for me.

It was desire most true: unattainable, untouchable, remote, yet
    imaginable, like a pair of lovers opening into one another,

a man's mouth making dove sounds, tiny purple blossoms overtaking
    their bodies, dark rose petals sliding up the inside of his leg,

red flowers, pink flowers, red lips, red thighs,
    His rise, he reaches for me...Who insisted that in this bright world

you would not be whole? No entrance, no end, no birds, no flowers,
    and luminous between you and splendor the thin cruel line of water.

The Blue Room
(Picasso)

I. What man would bathe a woman in such blue

II. Turn even the water blue   her skin blue

III. What does the color blue mean to you

IV. Was the woman blue before Picasso made her blue

V. Are you blue

VI. Once in the Gulf of Mexico I got sucked under my face turned blue

VII. This room is blue this is the blue room

VIII. Not only love is blue   everything is blue

IX. Picasso said

Sojourn

Gray houses facing the sea.
You might remember those mornings of fog and mist,
the in-rush of sea foam, waves,
the broken weathervane on the dilapidated house
striking the red-tiled roof. Seabirds flying over the sandbar,
white, like the inland birds seen surrounding cows.
One bird in particular was beautiful coming in,
sailing at a constant height, then dropping a few feet
on extended wings until the next fall, tier-like,
down to the shallow water and silver waves.
Your wrists inside little cuffs of jewelry
motioning in the air and your face
the one I carry with me into the present.
Iridescent scales washed up around our feet, the invertebrate shells
of random shapes and colors
from that tumultuous and caged sea
we watched all afternoon, wordless.
Your hand fell into mine. I perished into the afternoon.
Then departure, tugboats sounding through water,
and the gates to the storefront windows being drawn down.
Years now since we pondered our lives by the sea
and where no shadow fell across us.

At the Port House

At night the old city below shimmers, the electrical lights
like faint stars (sometimes you can make out
a few familiar streets, the cathedral
towering above the café). Millions of years ago
all this would be underwater at a sea depth impenetrable to light,
even the high cliff where I am standing now
an ocean floor, host only to blind things, albino…

You were never so present as in this absence.

Night, and a stray cat crossing the open yard.
Night, and a broken wheel of planets and stars.
Dark trees swaying, ghost-like,
as if inhabited by souls (a childhood memory).

Then a sudden flight of birds, laughter in the distance,
dark freckles across a passing stranger's face
shaped like your own.

This is what you've become—
the flower's throat, the neighbor's hand—

everywhere
in tenuous, beautiful resemblance.

♦

Amulet

Then beauty became inseparable from sadness.
An earring perhaps, found in a drawer among papers.
Or walking at sundown, watching
the starlings over the rooftops.
It was as if his failed desires had made it so,
or the loss of his own beauty, or youth.
He'd be pierced with longing after passing
a stranger's mysterious face
or a wild rose seen from a car window.
If only there was something—
an anodyne, an amulet, a chrysalis.
In the wind, he heard bells from a distant cathedral.
Two seagulls were fading above the bay.

Continuum

And often it was frightening for him to look inward
into the complexities of his mind.
Sometimes he would discover an immense sadness
there, hidden beneath his daily thoughts
like a suicide kept underwater by heavy, unseen currents.
He'd carry it unknowingly among the myriad streets, faces.
It would surface in his quiet contemplations at night
as he walked among the fish houses and empty wharves.
He'd watch, along the river's edge, how the water
would push forth hollow, drowned things.
And it was evident in all the fadings of beauty.
He'd hear, late at night, a hand falling in intervals
as though from a clock hidden somewhere inside his house.
There was a lazy continuum between his days,
and the beloved remained distant.

Annunciation Street

He recalled mornings when the city was veiled by clouds and fog,
a steady rain falling and a quiet holiness that seemed to be everywhere
but couldn't be explained, like the sudden stillness of a cat
while cleaning its fur under a window through which the sun poured.
He recalled the twenty roses outside the window standing perfectly in air
like souls come back, he thought, as if to say
passage into something else was possible after all.
His afternoons increased like honey.
There were clouds and silences,
wild doves plunging in the blue.

Self-Portrait in New Orleans

I see my reflection in the watery windows of houses
and my reflection is bent as if in water.
I see the heavy pink blossoms held up among branches
and see no reflection of myself
in the blossoming. My identity seems strange to me—
vast, in flux, always changing,
as if I don't know who I am
because I'm no longer the person I was before.

I go down Laurel Street
among houses of the poor, among dilapidated streets
full of lost trumpets and broken moonlight.
And the houses are full of absences
because people slip under, cross over.
I might have just witnessed the face of a deranged man,
or passed a certain wharf
where massive ships unload a freight of ash and bones.

I go in search of meaning and resemblances;
I cross streets that turn into swift-moving parades
of confetti, horses, and men,
where the spirit can't blossom anymore;
where the heart grows indifferent from daily life.

I know the heaviness and tedium in things

such as houses and railway yards—
things that have existed in one place for a long time;
the fatigue in seeing, in images—
bankers, cats, advertisements, laundry detergents,
priests nodding off in city buses,
and ladies beneath pink parasols.

Now the movement of tugboats leaving the wharves,
and a flock of herons nearly invisible on a hill.
Nothing in the heart except desire
in neighborhoods among scattered autumn leaves.

November Days

To have traveled this far
only not to believe in the romances anymore;
to have come to this city of wharves and warehouses along the river
only not to feel the mysteries anymore;
to go up humid streets laden with bougainvillea and banana trees,
or past the Victorian, dilapidated
mansions on the avenues with only a diminished, faded self.
How should one live in this age?
Steamboats go out to the Gulf here,
and, at evening, magenta-colored clouds hurry along the river
like deranged, abstract animals.
I go up streets and my reflection's lost in storefront windows
among others. Already the soft lights
appear across the river. Already
the thread of my life is unwinding on its spool.

The Snowflake

It came suddenly, unexpectedly. There were five gold lilies
beside the open window where he sat cutting his toenails.
Outside he heard many doves, a republic of notes
falling from his neighbor's rooftop.
It could be said that the man resembled a lily
(it was then that he resembled a lily),
or his face did, or his heart, just as each cut nail resembled
a crescent moon. The clouds seemed to be raining.
But they looked more like mountains. It fell everywhere,
this notion, as the snowflake entered the room
and vanished upon landing on a chair, the finality of death.

Lafayette Cemetery No. 1

There were tombs taller than I,
tombs with small votives and plastic flowers,
tombs with angels on them with lowered heads.
Someone said that inside those vaults
lay the bones of an entire family—
a daughter's bones resting on top her grandfather's
bones, and so on. Walking among the dead that afternoon,
sometimes a sentence would come to mind and I would say it,
or a solitary woman would pass by crossing herself,
or a blackbird would circle, light on a far grave.
Do souls travel?
Do they pass like candles into other worlds?
I asked these questions in New Orleans, beneath Japanese magnolias
shedding heavy pink blossoms among the graves.

Come

They say you have your reasons

That you will come
loud like a helicopter
for those
they say
you love

But I
the bloodworm
the sheep tick
the blow fly
the jimson weed
the spotted leaf
the crabgrass
the moccasin
the black back jackal
the nagana
the spider

have come to expect your absence

First Lines of an Unfinished Elegy

When he moved among flowers they opened for him

When he sat on a chair, reading, or when he motioned to the stars
he could level you with his eyes; they contained the sadness of children

In a crowd he always stood out as the most solemn, the most beautiful

If you unclasped his hands, you'd find the light of the universe

The Many Stars

Because in your passage you have not become laurel,
rose, or hyacinth,
and because stars are incomprehensible formulations of gas
(which last night peacefully lit up the revolving sky)
and not the souls of those departed,
I do not know what has become of you.
Even here it seemed you existed on a different plane,
moving over everything self-sufficient as roses,
silent, intelligent, austere, with a masculine indifference
which suddenly would erupt into laughter.
The cruelty of your passing is that nothing changed
when it seemed as if everything had changed. You were not
the center around which the invisible axis
turned; no rain of flowers fell over
everything; the irises did not shut, did not close,
your thread unraveling, unraveling…
Yesterday in a field of bright copper
I saw an old abandoned house
made of limestone with the roof half sagging in, half gone—
four ceiling beams exposed to the sky
like a large animal's rib cage. When I pulled out one small stone
wedged between the mortar, the slightest
pressure of my fingers
turned that piece of house to dust.

Horses of Cerrillos

Everything is steady here, punctuated by moments
of excitement, boredom, and laughter.
The forsythia in the yard is bent over with frost.
The frightening moths of last summer I keep finding in the pages
of old books, crushed.
This morning I struggled to paint in red and silver
the many rooftops on the hill
which through a skewed perspective appeared stacked
on top of one another. Then a plank in the sky
must have broken because suddenly there was snow,
much snow. The landscape is sad
here, I think, because much suffering occurs
in these towns strewn with pinion trees, fallen telephone poles,
rabbits, coyotes, and wooden crosses
on the rims of abandoned iron ores.
The horses are silent as they move through
New Mexico. I have the photograph of you
as a boy trying not to laugh beneath
the old cottonwood tree at the house.
It was springtime then;
the roses were beginning to come through.
Last night, I saw stars washed on a windowpane, distorted
by a soft, steady rain. Days like these
one does not know *how*
to hope, Alfonso; best to feel that you've already

become cloud, lily root,
or this snow falling now through many worlds.

1909-1999

That Other River

I heard one autumn
a great migration of birds passing along the coast
in the western sky

They made a river
                that mirrored that other river
    made of time and dust—

the fall of Rome, Shakespeare, the twelve Apostles,
a scent of lilac,
mathematics, stars, bone, the sea—

a passing kingdom, nameless

Snow

It is winter.

My father is eight years old,
his foot caught deep in the crotch of a sycamore.

He twists and falls,
waits alone across the field.

Can you see his face,
the white bone poked through his leg,
the snow?

Early Morning, Winter

Turning from the window down the hallway into the room
    I saw my father   But it was not my father
Only my face in the mirror watching him

The Junkyard

My father told me a story I will try
to tell you what he said

I do not know how old he was
he was looking for something

in a junkyard somewhere
maybe in Mexico

I cannot remember
& out of nowhere

rain broke from the clouds
above him

& lightning struck beside him
He found an old blue bus

lying on its side
twisted & bent

as if dying
an old blue bus

that he crawled into
for cover

My father said
the strangest thing happened

he felt his hand resting
on a book

that he had never read before
about an old man

& the ark he built
before a flood

that happened once
the book said

Then suddenly it
stopped it stopped

& the storm & the lightning
went back inside the clouds

& my father carried the book
the whole way home

as though it were
the exact thing

he went there looking for

Seven

My father holds a knife

through my hair
into the door frame
above my head

Father says
I've grown a foot this year

Later
we eat cake and ice cream
laugh
watch TV

I fall asleep
in a new pair of gold pajamas

Snow ticks all night at my window

I hear even it too saying
Happy birthday

House

for my mother and father

There's more beauty
you said
chasing a dream
than obtaining one
& we had our
sea of dreams
we dreamt
of buying a house
near an ocean
or a riverbed
a house
in the mountains
with a balcony
upstairs
for stargazing
but we lived
in the city
with thick haze
and the glare
of streetlights
so we cut
from newspapers
a few stars
and a full moon
to paste

on the windows

as we

softly

began our lives

Seascape

An unexpected snowfall in a rented room by the sea
where sea horses slumber and drowned grasses
sway in perpetual current. The lichen-covered fence with the lovers'
initials carved in it; the myriad shells, fish bones,
the lighthouse swinging its light overhead,
the snow in the air turning to mist
and the mist falling into the sea.
You lean toward the window, making out
two birds, two shadows, sailing up and over
the carnival tent and Ferris wheel,
then their slow descent
to the wooden pier lashed by waves.
You walk to the other window
where, outside, grasses lie flat on dunes,
blown over by wind and rain,
and smoke rises from the few houses
visible on the hill. Still, the questions that riddle you
are unanswerable, mercurial, feminine;
still the desires of the body
are yesterday's desires, which never leave,
and love remains distant, distant.
This tide, this sea, sapphire, ascendant.
You stand at the window and watch waves
and ghostly apparitions, a low ceiling of moving clouds and rain.

Mythic Fragment

One afternoon Penelope rises from the gigantic table
strewn with fabric. And spotting through her window
a winding path beyond a clearing in the green woods,
she chooses to go. The wind as she leaves
the house tightens her dress across her body.
But there's a choice to be made—*If I leave my chamber
and my husband returns and is made to search for me,
then I will be guilty of returning the injury befallen me.*
Therefore, she goes. There are the recognizable cries of birds
perched now on the latticed branches above her,
the exotic fragrances the wind has thrown like spices
through her window as she slept. These woods
are amazing as they are, filled with descending shafts
of white light, a foyer possible for her. Yet nothing
prevents her fright that Odysseus has drowned, or worse,
has made a nest high between the legs of another's body.
Why can't the purple flowers tucked here save her?
Why won't Odysseus return? Her dress is a heavy one
as it is, embroidered with golden birds, a few leaves, and a star.

The Missing One

Where window curtains are blown back revealing an ivory room,
a woman keeps bending down, and bending down again,
as though bowing to some unseen presence, or excusing herself
from a crowd of men who might hurt or leave her.
She is gathering beads spilled from her broken necklace.
But every now and then she stands up straight, collects herself, counts
the beads, discerns them—actions she never really took while
the necklace was still around her neck—until she realizes
that the largest bead is missing, the middle one.
Then she no longer searches for it, because deep within her
she discovers that which was always missing in her,
that which is always missing, a notion, perhaps, or
a lightness, like this piece of broken string that hangs from her fingers
and which she now studies.

after Ritsos

Nude Blue III, 1952

(Matisse)

Perhaps she is dreaming of the sea,
of blue snow,
or an island of women sunbathing on a beach.

Or perhaps she is crying,
revealing the blue of
sadness, of love.

Notice now how embarrassed she seems,
naked,
brushing back her hair in blue laughter.

The Sleepers

Such a private thing done in public:
these three undergraduates asleep on the sofas
in the east wing of the University Library.
One's a perfect model for Balthus—
confidently asleep on his back, his head tilted
back, jaw open, left arm flung over
(perhaps he is dreaming of riding horses).
The second one has lifted the bottom
of his white button-down shirt,
revealing a forest of tangled belly hair,
and his right hand is spread across his heart
like one who walks surprisingly into a room
full of friends. But the third one's arm is draped across her face
so that you have to tilt your head sideways
to see that her mouth is open
almost imperceptibly to the room.
Red hair tumbles downward in curls across the sofa,
and her chest rises and falls with each breath.
Soon the library turns dark. I mark my pages with a star.
I can't even imagine it anymore: not being
undone by the beauty of others.

Reckonings

I have the face of my father   I've seen stars so distant
that they perished before I saw them

I've known the unjust, the broken, the vanquished
I've seen eyes that were dead

I was given the sadness of my elders, it was my card
I lived alone

I was the luminous spider web beneath a railing
that no one saw

I have a notion of God
that no one taught me   that I am blessed
like a grove of lilies swaying on His hand

I dwelled in the house of oblivion
I walked among the bones and the flowers

Now Many Days

Now many days
pass and nothing memorable happens,
and the days become forgotten, blurred,
too remote to be recalled individually. Yesterday
I saw flower blossoms scattered around my feet from an unseen
tree, as if they fell high up from space.
I felt poured out like waves of water
against an island's shore. Your eyes I remember
are the color of blue lupine,
and your hair as you sat beneath your window,
reading, sighing in intervals,
was streaked auburn and maple-brown.
Often I thought of you as going down,
alone, into a dark interior,
from which there was no rescue,
from which you couldn't turn to anyone for help.
One afternoon in Rothko's Chapel
we stood together
staring at Rothko's last, large, dark paintings that he finished
just before his suicide.
They were representations, I thought,
of dark interiors and souls,
lit almost solely
by the natural light
coming in from the museum's ceiling. I remember you being struck by

the constant play of changing light
on the walls, and sometimes a sudden brightness
would overtake the rooms and the dark canvases…

Today a light rain falls, and clouds hurry along the Mississippi
where a few afternoon stragglers have come to stare at the vast,
vacant river with their faces expressionless like stone.
Wherever you are, I remain
your brother
in this vortex of disappearing days.

To Borges

Dreamer of tigers, Argentine, twice-married, librarian,
now dust: forty years ago you lived
in this city, a visiting professor. Local images:
a beautiful yet dangerous-looking young woman
on the forlorn Drag, feral cats in the State's
official rose garden, and my favorite—
in the otherwise intolerable heat of August
the white rain lilies
suspended in my yard like little floating stars.
When did my hands begin to look so old?
I never paid much attention to them
until last night when I saw the hands of my father
at the end of my wrists. Gone are those boyish hands
that once sharpened a wooden blade beneath stars,
or those that anxiously unbuttoned a girl's
blouse for the first time; absent too are those hands
used in a wedding ceremony five years ago
in a chapel filled with candles and flowers.
And no longer live those flowers like blue water
spilling over the clasped hands of the bride
of snow. And it was you above all poets, Borges,
who knew the infinite temporality of things
who sang of unremembered roses,
forgotten patios, the wiped-out
Saxons, comets…

Actions, thoughts, passions—doesn't everything recede now
into memory, which itself fades in clarity,
blurred like the white eyes of the blind?
And so it is not with much protest this afternoon
when I think of your dying. Like the rest of us
you've gone on ahead—
in the way of all flowers, civilizations, and dreams.
But your words I carry with me into the present—
into this world of passing, world of oblivion. *I too
am a whim of time, that shifty element.*

La Nouvelle Orleans

Long, languid summer afternoons

when everything returns
to stillness—

the bougainvillea withers on its vine;
only the slow turning of a fan

is witnessed on an abandoned balcony
on Arabella Street.

Whatever has remained of the Holy
has disappeared,

as though carried off by the vagabonds
who whitewashed

the cathedral
but haven't been seen for days.

Black thunderclouds blossom overhead;
already I want to fade into something better.

Your sorrow remains, and the ache.

Marine

A huge blue sail was flapping above the horizon.
The oak leaves remained still, burned white.
Scent of sea water, a constellation

of sand on my ankle. In the distance,
the nets rising and falling.

Your mouth was embroidered with mine.

♦

Notes

"Window in Nice, 1919" is after a painting of the same name by Henri Matisse

"Ovid's Narcissus" derives some language from Ovid's *Metamorphoses*

"The Blue Room" is after a painting of the same name by Pablo Picasso

"The Many Stars" and "Horses of Cerrillos" are written in memory of Alfonso Chavez, my grandfather, of Santa Fe, New Mexico

"The Missing One" is a reworking of Yannis Ritsos's poem entitled "Broken String"

"Nude Blue III, 1952" is after a painting of the same name by Henri Matisse

"Now Many Days" is for Matthew North Harvey

"To Borges" references Jorge Luis Borges, who lived in Austin, Texas, for a brief time

Travis Ian Smith currently lives in New Orleans, where he teaches writing and literature as an adjunct instructor at Tulane University in the School of Continuing Studies. His poems have appeared in numerous literary journals such as *Borderlands: Texas Poetry Review*, *The Grasslands Review*, *The Red River Review*, *The Texas Observer*, *Sun Poetic Times*, and *Volpe*. He holds degrees from Baylor University and Texas State University, where he earned an MFA in Creative Writing.

www.ingramcontent.com/pod-product-compliance
Lightning Source LLC
Chambersburg PA
CBHW031210090426
42736CB00009B/864